MEDITATIONS FOR THE SIX DAYS OF HOLY WEEK

C. Alton Robertson

CSS Publishing Company, Inc., Lima, Ohio

MEDITATIONS FOR THE SIX DAYS OF HOLY WEEK

Scripture quotations are from the *Revised Standard Version of the Bible,* copyrighted 1946, 1952 ©, 1971, 1973, Division of Christian Education of the National Council of the Churches of Christ in the USA. Used by permission.

This book is available in the following formats, listed by ISBN:
    0-7880-0731-9 Book
    0-7880-0889-7 Mac
    0-7880-0890-0 IBM 3 1/2
    0-7880-0891-9 Sermon Prep

PRINTED IN U.S.A.

*This book is dedicated to the memory of
Sadao Watanabe, stencil-print artist and
my friend, who died on 8 January 1996.
"May light perpetual shine upon him."*

These meditations were first used in daily services at Tokyo Union Church during Holy Week, 1960. The setting was the church basement — cleared, somewhat stark in its bareness.

Persons gathered between 7:15 and 7:30 a.m. in silence. At 7:30 each morning, a pre-circulated prayer was said in unison. Fifteen minutes of silence followed during which the recommended scriptures could be read and private meditation and prayers could be made.

At 7:45 each morning, Peter spoke, and his monologue was followed by silence. The service ended each day at 8:00 a.m. as one of the participants, who had been selected beforehand, led the group in a prayer of dismissal.

Scriptural quotations are from the Revised Standard Version of The Bible. The reference to Jesus stopping the people from carrying their water pots through the Temple is from the Phillips translation of the New Testament.

FOREWORD

We often know something in our minds, but do not know it with our hearts. Shakespeare in *Hamlet* spoke of "knowing feelingly," and it is exactly this kind of knowing that we must somehow obtain if the Bible and our Christian heritage are to live for us. We must relive the accounts. Imagination is indispensable for we must enter the bodies of the persons and live through the situations — smelling what they smelled, hearing what they heard, feeling what they felt. Until this happens, we cannot really know a thing; we cannot fully understand.

For this week of morning devotions, I would like to relive Holy Week with you. I have chosen to enter the body of Peter, the brother of Andrew, who was with Jesus throughout his ministry. Will you join me in this attempt to know Holy Week? Will you become Peter with me?

MONDAY

Time: Morning
Place: Bethany

Recommended readings: Matthew 21:1-11
                                         Mark 11:1-11
                                         Luke 19:28-44
                                         John 12:12-36

Yesterday as we were approaching Bethphage and Bethany just outside the city of Jerusalem, the Master sent Thomas and Matthew ahead to get an ass. How strange, I thought. We had been on the road for over thirty days, and he had walked along with us. Today we were completing our trip and entering the city of Jerusalem. Would he ride in on an ass? What a strange thing to do.

It was strange — the whole affair — for, you see, our entry wasn't like a group of Passover Week pilgrims arriving in the city, eager to reach the bazaar, to meet friends and relatives whom they hadn't seen since last year, scurrying around to find a place to stay during the crowded week. Frankly, as it turned out, our entrance into the city was more like the return of an exiled monarch, the triumphant entry of a king. Yet not really like a king; for that little, brown ass wasn't like a white stallion, and Jesus' simple, seamless robe had no trace of royal purple in it. And my old, faded cloak on top of those we placed on the ass to make a more comfortable seat was certainly far from a kingly saddle with silver trim.

It was quaint — and different. Some might have thought it shabby; and, in its elements, I suppose it was — if one had eyes for just the elements. The Master, however, even on that ass, was himself. There was no attempt at pretending grandeur. He sat very straight with his head slightly bowed — a mingling of sorrow and love on his face.

After we got him seated on the ass and began to move toward the city, the people began to put their cloaks in the road to make a carpet. Then they began to break branches off the trees. They waved them in the air as Jesus passed, and they shouted, "Hosanna. Blessed is he who comes in the name of the Lord." "God save the Son of David!" "Hurrah for the coming kingdom of our father David." "There is peace in Heaven and glory on high!"

Frankly, I thought of silencing the crowd. After all, it was only a couple of weeks ago at Caesarea-Philippi that, after I had answered his question concerning his identity with "Thou art the Christ, the son of the Living God," he had told us very emphatically that we should not tell anyone that he was the Christ. I could have silenced that crowd, you know. I could have simply stopped the procession and shouted at them to keep their tongues silent. I was considering doing it (though I couldn't understand why the Master himself didn't) when some Pharisees in the crowd approached him and shouted, "Master, restrain your disciples!" Jesus simply looked at them, and then he said, "I tell you that if they kept quiet, the stones in the road would burst into cheers." The Pharisees drew back. And so did I. So the time had come to let it be known. Our Master is the Christ.

The crowd did grow silent at one point though. We turned a bend in the road. You know the place — there where you come out of the mountains and below you Jerusalem becomes visible. All spread out like a big, white shell. After the long trip, it is always such a good sight because you know for sure that you have almost made it. Well, yesterday, when we turned that bend and there lay Jerusalem, the city of our fathers, the city of the Temple, a strange silence came over the crowd. And, then, I realized what was happening. Jesus had stopped the ass. He sat very quietly, looking at the city below. And then he was weeping.

There was nothing anyone could do. We just stood and looked, too. And because I know the Master and I could feel how he felt, at least to some extent, I found tears coming to my eyes, too. I'm not sure how long we stood there transfixed before he spoke. But then his voice pierced the silence as he said, "Ah, if you only knew, even at this eleventh hour, on what your peace depends — but you cannot see it ... You did not know when God Himself was visiting you."

TUESDAY

Time: Morning
Place: The Temple courtyard

Recommended readings: Matthew 21:12-17
                                               Mark 11:15-19
                                               Luke 19:45-46

As I think now of Sunday and the humble procession into the city and contrast it with yesterday, it is almost as if my Master is two persons. And yet they are congruent. Each is a part of the same whole. What Sunday lacked in action, yesterday provided. You've heard about it, I'm sure. Everyone in Jerusalem is talking about it, for never before has such a thing occurred.

The scribes and elders of the Temple are furious. They are demanding that the Chief Priest get Jesus out of the city. There are even rumors that they want him to be killed. He knows this, and yet there he sits, right over there, surrounded by people, talking quietly, answering questions, questioning. He is attracting larger crowds than the magicians and bazaars. He is receiving a larger audience than the Temple officials who have scheduled lectures.

Never has a Passover Week been quite like this. It has become something of an annual festival, a time of celebration. The significance of the Passover event has long been neglected. The exodus of our families from Egypt and their covenant with God are some vague events of the past that have become so encrusted with tradition and interpretation that most of us are not quite sure of their meaning. Celebrating Passover is simply our custom. The Temple is something vaguely important, and sacrifices are one of those obligations we can't neglect and feel right about — even if we're not really sure that they have meaning.

Well, yesterday we came back into the city after spending the night in Bethany. And the Master came directly here to the Temple.

We had been here the day before, and he had seemed disquieted, though he said nothing. But yesterday he walked in somewhat commandingly, intent on doing something that had to be done, and yet not with any sense of glee or taste for the job at hand. He wasn't like a sergeant or a sneering landlord taking delight in high-handing his subordinates or tenants. He moved quickly, yet with humility. He spoke with the assurance of authority, the conviction of truth, and yet with the undergirding essence of love.

Yes, he drove out those who were buying and selling here. He actually overturned the tables of the money changers and the benches of the dove sellers. There was confusion. There was noise. Animals and birds were loose. Money rolled on the floor. Benches clattered. Tables crashed. People cried out in protest. And over it all, I heard the Master say, "Doesn't the Scripture say, 'My house shall be called a house of prayer for all nations?' But you have turned it into a thieves' kitchen!"

He even stopped the people who were carrying their water pots through the Temple and commanded them to stop such a practice. It was in this that I saw the basic truth. The money changers, the dove sellers — that was obvious. That we all recognize. But carrying a water pot through the Temple? We all do. It's usual and certainly not the same as the money changers, the dove sellers, the bartering, and business. But it's the same — the same. And we are all involved. The Temple has become a part of the city, like a bank, a store, a kitchen in the home. The sacred is handled in ignorance unknowingly. The holy has become mundane. We wear our shoes everywhere and never recognize the holy ground we trample on.

I reread the holy scripture last night after we were back in Bethany — the section in 1 Kings 8 and 9 where King Solomon dedicated the first temple after its completion. In addressing the people of Israel at the time of the dedication, Solomon said, " 'Now the Lord has fulfilled his promise which he made ... and I have built the house for the name of the Lord, the God of Israel.' Then Solomon prayed, 'O Lord, God of Israel, there is no God like thee, in heaven above or on earth beneath, keeping covenant and showing steadfast love to thy servants who walk before thee with all their heart ... But will God indeed dwell on the earth? Behold, heaven and the highest heaven cannot contain thee; how much less this house which I have built! Yet have regard to the prayer of thy servant and to his supplication, O Lord my God, ... that thy eyes may be open night and day toward this house, the place of which thou hast said, 'My name shall be there.' And the Lord said to him, 'I have heard your prayer and your supplication, which you have made before me; I have consecrated this house which you have built, and put my name there forever; my eyes and my heart will be there for all time.' "

I reread these holy scriptures, and I realized, perhaps for the first time, the true import assigned to the Temple. It is more than a place where priests kill animals, where men in long robes, looking very austere and pious, make their home. It is more than simply the heritage of us Jews. It is a place where God indwells, a place where his name is found. And I thought about the day in Samaria when'the Master talked with the woman. She had tried to raise a dispute over the proper place of worship — at this Temple or at Mount Gerizim — and Jesus had answered that the time was soon coming when people would worship God neither in this Temple nor on that mountain because, he had declared, "God is Spirit and those who worship him must worship in spirit and truth."

And yet, if the Temple is where our worship was to have centered and we have so perverted it and made it something so minus spirit and truth, so corrupt, how will we be able to make the transition to the more difficult, more unfocused worship that Jesus proposes? He had to drive out those money changers, those dove sellers, and he had to stop us from carrying our water pots through the Temple. The attempt at purification had to be made if we are to understand and gain some sense of the holiness of the Holy, the sacredness of the Sacred, the awesomeness of the Awesome. If you and I are to approach God ourselves, we must know what it is we do.

And yesterday when the confusion had ended and things were quiet, after the money changers and dove sellers had retreated and the people had taken their water pots away, right here in the Temple, the blind and the lame came to him, and he healed them. All in the same afternoon. And this is my Lord. He **is** the Christ.

WEDNESDAY

Time: Evening
Place: Bethany

Recommended readings: Matthew 21:23—24:2
                                       Mark 11:27—13:2
                                       Luke 19:45-46

We did not go into the city today. The people are probably wondering why. They surely must have gathered in the Temple to meet with Jesus once more. They are probably wondering if something has gone wrong. The Master didn't tell us why; he simply said that today we would remain in Bethany. He has spent much time reading the holy scriptures — especially the prophet Isaiah. And, now, he is off by himself, walking in the evening.

The opposition is growing. Yesterday, even in the midst of all the people, the Chief Priests, scribes, and elders questioned his authority and even said, "Who gave you permission to do what you are doing?" He did not become defensive. He simply countered with a question to them, which made them turn away. He asked them whether John's baptism came from heaven or was purely human. He said that if they would answer that, then he would declare to them his authority. They could not answer; they could only argue with one another. There in the midst of the people who know that John was a prophet, they had to take the position of the undeclared, to accept the flabby distinction of men without a conviction or stand worth defending.

The Pharisees, whom he has openly criticized and whose hypocrisy he has unmasked, are determined that he fall. They, with the Herodians, approached him with a question about paying taxes to Caesar. They coated their question with flattery and false words; and he, with his penetrating gaze, simply slashed them and sent them away staggered with the declaration, "Give to Caesar what belongs to Caesar and to God what belongs to God."

15

Then the Sadducees, who deny that there is any resurrection, came with an obviously contrived question concerning it. With calmness and only a few words, without argument or name calling, he silenced them.

The Pharisees, who, as everyone knows, hate the Sadducees, were delighted when they heard how he had stopped them in their tracks. So they rallied once more and came in force to hear one of their experts in the Law put a test question to him concerning the greatest commandment.

As I saw these, the religious leaders of our day, scheming and plotting, trying to trick him, coming back time after time, I was filled with disgust and fury. Had it been me, I would have called their hand and denounced them. They were sneaky, obviously insincere, openly malicious. And yet Jesus listened to their questions, provided wise answers with patience, and utilized their presence and questions in clarifying his teaching to the crowds that were gathered around him.

That all these groups are opposed to the Master, we knew. But what became openly apparent yesterday is that they are getting together. Divided, none of them can get rid of him, and they know it. So he, a common enemy, as it were, is drawing them together despite their many differences and ancient history of animosity. All Evil is gathering to stamp out Good. And as this Evil unites and cloaks itself in darkness, it looks large and foreboding. And there sits the Good, openly teaching in the courtyard of the Temple — a humble ex-carpenter. One wonders what the end will be.

I love this man. When I hear him so calmly denounce the scribes and Pharisees — whitewashed tombs, he called them (looking fine on the outside, but inside full of dead men's bones and all kinds of rottenness) — I can't help but feel very proud of him. I have sometimes wondered if I did right to leave my wife and children back in Capernaum with her mother while I tramped over the country with this Jesus. But this week, I am convinced that I did right.

We are all becoming certain that he will never leave Jerusalem alive this week. Exactly what it will mean, I'm not sure. We, too, may die with him. I tell myself that I'm willing, but I really don't know if I could. I know the commandments that the Master has been emphasizing — love God and love neighbor as self. I felt the impact of the Master's commendation of the poor widow yesterday as he sat watching the people make their offerings; and, though her gift was small, it was her all. But one's very life? Death and dying nobly are grand to talk about when they are impersonal. But when they may be just over another day, one stops and thinks. I told Jesus once that I would follow him even unto death. But I didn't expect him to die.

THURSDAY

Time: Evening
Place: The Upper Room

Recommended readings: Matthew 26:1-13
                                         Mark 14:1-9

As I sit here at this table waiting for the Master to arrive, I cannot help but think about the other night at dinner when that woman came in. Tuesday night it was, and we were at the home of Simon the leper. During the meal (I was talking with James at the time, and we were reviewing the day and all that had taken place), my head was turned from the Master, who sat to the right of our host, but, catching a look of surprise on James' face, I turned, and there was a woman pouring perfume on the Master's head. We all sat somewhat stunned by this unusual behavior, and I could not help but notice that it was very costly spikenard perfume — the kind my wife has always wanted but has never had. It was in an alabaster flask, and the woman had actually broken the neck of the flask.

As my surprise gave way to clearer vision and the connection of the perfume to my wife faded, I could look at the woman. Her face was radiant. This was her gift, perhaps her only treasure. How long had she saved this flask of perfume? How many of her neighbors had observed it in her home and been impressed and obviously envious? How often had she carefully rationed the number of drops she dare use? And here she was, pouring it out — lavishing it on the head of a man. Her prized possession vanishing in one extravagant moment. But such a moment. They call me insensitive, and I suppose they're right, but I couldn't miss the wholesomeness, the deep emotion of this act. But some did. Around me, various ones began to mutter, "What a wicked waste of such costly perfume." "That could have been sold and the money given to the poor." "Such a foolish woman." "Why didn't someone stop her?"

But the Master understood. He knew her feeling, and he reached out to protect her from the assault of the disgruntled. "Let her alone," he said. "Why must you make her feel uncomfortable?" Then looking at her and back to us, he added, "She has done a beautiful thing for me." With true appreciation in his voice, he said that. "She has done a beautiful thing for me." And she had. I felt it down deep inside of me. "You have the poor with you always and you can do good to them whenever you like, but you will not always have me. She has done all she could — for she has anointed my body for burial before the time. I assure you that wherever the Gospel is preached throughout the whole world, this deed of hers will also be told in memory of her."

Some obviously couldn't understand his attitude, but I longed to know that woman better and to hear of the experiences she has had that made her perform this act. What had the Master done for her? Out of what deep sense of gratitude and love had this extravagant deed come?

And, now, tonight we have dinner again. But this is the Passover meal. So long ago it was when our people, the slaves in Egypt, killed the lambs and put the blood on their mantles so that the angel of death would pass over. A life sacrificed that life might continue. Blood spilled in an effort to save. God was choosing our ancestors for his people to serve him in the world. And tonight we will mark this ancient feast and seek to renew in our hearts the covenant our people have with God.

Here before me is the roasted lamb, the hyssop, the unleavened bread. John and I came in early this morning to make ready for this meal tonight. Andrew and James were the next to arrive. We felt it unsafe to come in from Bethany all together; so alone or in pairs we have made our way to this upper room. Each of us is aware that to the Master this evening and this meal together are very important. He has gone to much trouble to see that it was arranged.

Tonight we shall mark the Passover in obedience to God's words to Moses, which our fathers have recited to us each year since our childhoods and now we recite, "It is the Lord's passover. For I will pass through the land of Egypt ... and I will smite all the firstborn in the land of Egypt, both man and beast; and on all the gods of Egypt I will execute judgments: I am the Lord. The blood shall be a sign for you, upon the houses where you are; and when I see the blood, I will pass over you, and no plague shall fall upon you to destroy you, when I smite the land of Egypt. This day shall be for you a memorial day, and you shall observe it as an ordinance forever ... And when your children say to you, 'What do you mean by this service?' you shall say, 'It is the sacrifice of the Lord's passover, for he passed over the houses of the people of Israel in Egypt....' "

And so it was that God spared the firstborn of Israel. And tonight we shall mark the Passover with the firstborn of God.

FRIDAY

Time: Late morning
Place: Pilate's yard

Recommended readings: Matthew 26:17—27:23
                                         Mark 14:12—15:15
                                         Luke 22:1— 23:23
                                         John 18:1-40

(Peter enters in a raincoat. He is obviously distraught.)
I cannot talk to you today. I don't want to see anyone.
(Peter turns to leave, then whirls as if responding to a question from the crowd and shouts.)
I don't know why I did it. I was sure I wouldn't when he warned me. For once I knew that the Master was wrong. That I would deny him? Not I.
Not I. Not I. But I did. Three times I did. "I never knew him." "I, one of his friends? Girlie, you must be wrong." With curses and oaths, I denied him. And then the cock crew, and he turned and looked toward me, and ... What had I done? Why? Why? How could I have done it? That look. Oh, that look. He knew. And so I fled.
They took him, you know. It was after dinner when we went to the Mount of Olives. He knew that it was going to happen, for I overhead him praying in the Garden of Gethsemane. He seemed in agony and great turmoil. It was as though he were wrestling with some great conflict within himself. I wanted to rush to him and offer my help; but instead *(pause)* I went to sleep.
A great crowd came to get him, armed with swords and staves. They came for him as though he were a criminal holding out in a do-or-die last stand. The torches they carried lit up the garden and made everything rather eerie and unreal. But it was real all right. There was Judas. Poor Judas. We both failed him last night, and the others, too. They all ran away. And there was Jesus completely

23

forsaken. Yes, it was real. And my sword was real, too, when I struck that man. And the Master rebuked me and restored the man's ear. His last words to me were words of rebuke.

It was terrible. They dragged him over half the city last night. First, they took him to the house of Annas, the former High Priest and father-in-law of Caiaphas. Then, they dragged him to Caiaphas' home. At each place and all along the way they insulted him and struck him and even spit on him. I saw it, and I felt it at first. But it was too much. It was terrible. "Tell me, prophet, who hit you?" "Ah, king, *(pttt)*."

Early this morning, they took him over to Pilate. But because this is Passover Week, they wouldn't go in. They might become contaminated. Pilate, however, was in no great rush to get entangled in religious disputes that are no concern of his; so, when he heard that Jesus was from Galilee, which is under Herod's jurisdiction, he sent them on to Herod.

Now Herod was delighted, I hear. And he joined in the jeering and scoffing — even to the point of dressing the Master in a gorgeous cloak and giving him a scepter. What mockery! What outlandish arrogance!

Then Herod sent him back here to Pilate, and there he is now. He's being tried. False witnesses are heaping up false accusations, and he is silent. The mob is being aroused to shout, "Crucify him! Crucify him!"

Oh, if only I could run to him. If only I could proclaim his innocence. If only I . . . I?

"I never knew him." "I never knew him." "I never knew him."

(Peter runs from the room.)

SATURDAY

Time: Early morning
Place: The house in Jerusalem

Recommended readings: Matthew 27:24-66
                                         Mark 15:16-47
                                         Luke 23:24-56
                                         John 19:1-42

It's over now. Why do you wait here? Three years shot. He's dead, you know. And buried. All hell came out yesterday and nailed him to a cross out at Golgotha. The Good had been too much; and though it required the exposure of all Evil, Evil risked the exposure in this one concerted effort to crush its common enemy. But no one will ever be able to deny Evil again; and no one who saw it in action there at Pilate's yard or on that mountain will ever be able to forget.

The Master once said that he was the Light of the World. Well, yesterday, that Light was put out, extinguished, switched off.

I can hardly bring myself to accept this, and I must keep saying, "It's over. It's over. Go home, Peter, old boy. There's nothing more to keep you here in Jerusalem."

But he was the Christ. I knew that he would have to clash with Evil someday, but I didn't anticipate this ending. Oh, my God, not this ending. I knew that Good and Evil would meet, but I didn't expect Evil to win.

AFTERWORD

So this was Holy Week. THIS IS HOLY WEEK. This is past? THIS IS PRESENT. This is Judeo-Christian history? THIS IS COSMIC EVENT.

This is not just a nice story, a recounting of a week in the life of a man. This is a universally significant event. And it is in the light of this life and these events that the Christian views history and life.

In the light of these events, the resurrection makes sense. It is power. It is God's victory. It is the conquest of Good over Evil. It is God's answer to OUR attempt to kill him. It is not an individual promise of life forever. It is a statement about all humans and all of life. Easter has no meaning apart from Good Friday. Power has no meaning apart from love. The joy of Easter cannot be grasped unless the lostness and despair of Holy Saturday are endured.

It is here that power and love emerge in true perspective so that we can speak of true power and true love and declare that they are inseparable.

www.ingramcontent.com/pod-product-compliance
Lightning Source LLC
Chambersburg PA
CBHW071809020426
42331CB00008B/2448